W9-COE-507

WE THE PEOPLE

The Battles of Lexington & Concord

by Lucia Raatma

Content Adviser: David F. Wood,
Curator, Concord Museum,
Concord, Massachusetts

Reading Adviser: Dr. Linda D. Labbo,
Department of Reading Education, College of Education,
The University of Georgia

COMPASS POINT BOOKS
Minneapolis, Minnesota

Compass Point Books
3109 West 50th Street, #115
Minneapolis, MN 55410

Visit Compass Point Books on the Internet at *www.compasspointbooks.com*
or e-mail your request to *custserv@compasspointbooks.com*

Photographs ©: Courtesy of the Director, National Army Museum, London, cover, 23; North
Wind Picture Archives, 4, 11, 19, 22, 24, 27, 30, 33, 34, 37, 39, 40; Hulton/Archive by Getty
Images, 5, 6, 8, 12, 13, 14, 35; Stock Montage, 9; Yale Center for British Art, Paul Mellon
Collection/Bridgeman Art Library, 16; Freelance Photography Guild/Corbis, 17; James P. Rowan,
18, 25, 41; Scala/Art Resource N.Y., 20; Smithsonian American Art Museum, Washington,
D.C./Art Resource, N.Y., 28; Bettmann/Corbis, 31.

Editors: E. Russell Primm, Emily J. Dolbear, and Catherine Neitge
Photo Researcher: Svetlana Zhurkina
Photo Selector: Linda S. Koutris
Designer/Page Production: Bradfordesign, Inc./Biner Design
Cartographer: XNR Productions, Inc.

Library of Congress Cataloging-in-Publication Data
Raatma, Lucia.
   The Battles of Lexington and Concord / by Lucia Raatma.
      v. cm.—(We the people)
   Includes bibliographical references and index.
Contents: With the world watching—In the American colonies—The famous ride—Shots fired in
Lexington—The Battle of Concord—Back to Boston—The revolution begins—Glossary—
Did you know?—Important dates—Important people.
   ISBN 0-7565-0490-2 (hardcover : alk. paper)
   ISBN 0-7565-1051-1 (paperback)
   1. Lexington, Battle of, Lexington, Mass., 1775—Juvenile literature. 2. Concord, Battle of,
Concord, Mass., 1775—Juvenile literature. [1. Lexington, Battle of, Lexington, Mass., 1775.
2. Concord, Battle of, Concord, Mass., 1775. 3. United States—History—Revolution,
1775–1783—Campaigns.] I. Title. II. Series: We the people (Compass Point Books)
   E241.L6 R33 2004
   973.3'311—dc21   2002155731

TABLE OF CONTENTS

NOTE: *In this book, words that are defined in the glossary are in* **bold** *the first time they appear in the text.*

THE SHOT HEARD ROUND THE WORLD

The Revolutionary War (1775–1783) was an important event for the American **colonies** and for the government of Great Britain. It was fought to give the colonies freedom from British rule, and it ultimately created the United States of America. The Revolutionary War was also important to other countries, too. It was the first such revolution in modern times. It inspired people around the world to stand up to governments that were not fair.

Colonists fought the British at Bunker Hill in Boston, Massachusetts, in 1775. It was a key Revolutionary War battle.

4

French citizens stormed the Bastille in Paris during the French Revolution in 1789.

France experienced a similar revolution soon after the American success. Other revolutions have since taken place in Central America, South America, Russia, and Asia. The world took note as the American colonists fought the British. For this reason, when a gunshot was fired in battle in Concord, Massachusetts, it was called "the shot heard round the world."

IN THE AMERICAN COLONIES

Settlers had been coming to the American colonies from England since the 1600s, building settlements in places like Jamestown, Virginia, and Plymouth, Massachusetts. For many years, the colonists were content to be part of the British Empire. During the 1760s, however, their feelings began to change.

Early settlers in America were initially content to remain under British rule.

BRITISH
NORTH AMERICA

Lake
Superior

Lake
Michigan

Lake
Huron

Lake Ontario

Lake Erie

(part of
Massachusetts)

N.H.

New
York

Concord
Mass.

Conn.

Lexington
Boston
Plymouth

Rhode
Island

Pennsylvania

New Jersey

Maryland

Delaware

Proclamation line of 1763

Virginia

Jamestown

North
Carolina

South
Carolina

Georgia

Atlantic
Ocean

British colonies, 1775

N
W E
S

0   100   200 miles

0   100   200 kilometers

The thirteen American colonies

7

The British government was in debt after a long war with France. King George III and the government realized that one way to earn money for the British treasury was to put a tax on certain goods sold in the colonies. These goods included sugar, newspapers, playing cards, and tea. Many colonists did not think that such taxes were fair. Because they had no voice in the British government, the colonists did not believe they should pay taxes to support it.

This engraving by Paul Revere shows the four sides of a monument built in Boston to celebrate the end of certain British taxes in 1766.

British soldiers arresting a Patriot shortly before the Revolutionary War

Soon some of the colonists, who called themselves

Patriots, began to talk among themselves about the problems

they were having with the British king. They formed

9

groups and discussed ways to deal with the taxes. In one case, a crowd of people in Boston began throwing sticks, snowballs, and rocks at British troops. They called out to the soldiers and dared them to fire their weapons. Finally, the soldiers did fight back and killed five colonists. This dark day in March 1770 came to be called the Boston **Massacre.**

Another act of protest was known as the Boston Tea Party. One night in December 1773, a group of Patriots disguised as Native Americans boarded three British ships that were anchored in Boston Harbor. They dumped several containers of British tea into the water, making sure that no taxes would be paid for those shipments. This act made King George III furious. He responded by asking **Parliament** to create tougher laws and by sending more British troops to Boston. The colonists began calling some of these laws the Intolerable Acts because they could not tolerate, or put up with, living under them.

An engraving of the Boston Massacre by Paul Revere

The First Continental Congress met in Philadelphia, Pennsylvania, to discuss ways to deal with the British.

In 1774, a group of colonial leaders met at the First Continental Congress. They talked of ways to deal with the British government. They considered cutting off all trade between the colonies and Great Britain, and some colonial leaders even spoke of war.

12

PATRIOTS PLAN FOR ACTION

By April 1775, tensions between the American colonists and the British troops had reached a high point. Patriots watched the movements of the British troops and tried to determine what they would do next. Staying in Lexington, Massachusetts, were two important leaders of the revolutionary movement—Samuel Adams and John Hancock.

Samuel Adams was an important Patriot leader.

13

John Hancock was a wealthy merchant who joined the Patriots
in their fight against the British.

Samuel Adams was a man whose father had been successful in business. Adams, on the other hand, did not have a mind for making money. His talents lay in organizing people. Adams had boldly spoken out against King George III, and he had helped plan the Boston Tea Party. In contrast to Adams, John Hancock was a rich **merchant.** Considered to be the wealthiest man in Massachusetts, Hancock dressed in fine clothes and lived in a fancy house. He opposed the laws of England because they were hurting his business. He joined the Patriots because he hoped to win the colonies' freedom and to bring back fair trade.

In Concord—a town not far from Lexington— the Patriots had hidden guns, gunpowder, and other weapons in case fighting broke out with the British. King George III had heard rumors about these supplies. He ordered General Thomas Gage, the British military governor of Massachusetts, to find and destroy the

15

General Thomas Gage was the British military governor of Massachusetts.

supplies before they could be used. In the streets of Boston, Patriot spies learned of General Gage's orders and spread the news to their leaders. A surprise plan was put into action.

THE FAMOUS RIDE

One well-known resident of Boston was Paul Revere. He made his living as a silversmith, and he was also a messenger for the Patriots. On the evening of April 18, 1775, Revere was asked to meet with Dr. Joseph Warren, a Patriot leader in the city. Warren told Revere to ride to Lexington to warn Samuel Adams and John Hancock that the British troops were coming. If any of the British saw Adams and Hancock, the Patriot leaders would be arrested for working against the king.

Paul Revere was a silversmith who warned Samuel Adams and John Hancock that the British were coming to arrest them.

17

A view of Old North Church as it looks today

Revere had been expecting this assignment. A few days earlier, he had arranged a special signal with someone at Christ Church (now called Old North Church) in Boston. One lantern would be hung in the tower if the British were marching out of Boston Neck on foot. Two lanterns would be hung if they were crossing Boston's Charles River to Cambridge, Massachusetts.

18

That night Revere learned from Warren that the troops were moving across the Charles River. The first thing he did was go to Christ Church and give instructions for the two-lantern signal. Next, he ran down to the Charles River, where he met up with two friends who rowed him across the river to Charlestown.

In Charlestown, Revere borrowed a horse from Deacon

Two lanterns in the church tower meant the British were moving across the Charles River.

19

MINUTE MAN

*Minutemen were Patriot soldiers who could be prepared to fight
the British in a minute.*

John Larkin and set out on a ride through the dark
countryside. He rode from house to house, waking
families and warning them that the British were
coming. Minutemen—who were so named because
they could be ready to fight in a minute if necessary—
quickly pulled on their boots and coats. They set out
for Concord, hoping to reach their hidden supplies
before the British found them.

Upon arriving in Lexington, Revere woke up
Adams and Hancock. He warned them of the arrival
of the British troops, and the two men quickly prepared
to leave. Revere then met with another messenger,
William Dawes, and with a doctor named Samuel
Prescott. The three men headed for Concord with their
message. Before long, however, they were stopped by
British soldiers and questioned. Dawes and Prescott
both managed to escape. The soldiers finally released
Revere, but they kept his horse. Revere had to return

to Lexington on foot. In the meantime, Prescott continued on to Concord, warning everyone along the way. He told them to wake up and be ready. The British were coming!

During his midnight ride, Paul Revere warned other Patriots that the British were marching to Concord.

22

SHOTS FIRED IN LEXINGTON

Lieutenant Colonel Francis Smith led the British troops out of Boston on that April night. His orders from General Gage were to march secretly to Concord and find the supplies the Patriots had hidden there. However, as Colonel Smith and his soldiers made their way into Lexington, he realized their plans had been discovered. Though it was not yet dawn, houses were lit and people were awake. The British march to Concord was no longer a secret.

Lieutenant Colonel Francis Smith commanded the British soldiers who were marching to Concord.

23

The British soldiers did not want to start a war, and the minutemen would have preferred to avoid violence, too. However, neither side wanted to give in. Wearing fancy

Minutemen and British soldiers met to fight on Lexington Green on April 19, 1775.

red uniforms and carrying shiny rifles, the British arrived in Lexington. On Lexington Green, they were met by American colonists. A few dozen minutemen dressed in farm clothes and holding old **muskets** seemed like no match for the hundreds of soldiers. For a time, the two sides just stared at each other. British Major John Pitcairn told the minutemen to give up their weapons and go home. The Patriots, led by Captain John Parker, did not move.

A statue of Captain John Parker in Lexington

The silent standoff continued until suddenly a shot was fired. Some people say it came from the British side, while others say it was from a minuteman's musket. No matter who fired that opening shot, it was just the first of many. Shots rang out on both sides while Major Pitcairn yelled for his men to stop. The shooting continued for five minutes, until the British soldiers finally heard the order to cease fire. When the fighting ended that early April morning in Lexington, eight minutemen were dead and ten were hurt. Only one British soldier had been hit.

Compared with battles in other wars, the fight at Lexington was a short one. For the participants in the Revolutionary War, however, the shots fired there were just the beginning.

THE BATTLE OF CONCORD

Under Colonel Smith's command, the British troops continued on their march to Concord from Lexington. However, Smith knew that the American colonists were on the move, too. More Patriots would soon hear about the battle at Lexington, and more minutemen would soon be armed and ready. So Smith sent messengers back to Boston and requested that additional troops join them in Concord.

A minuteman prepares for battle with the help of his family.

27

Members of the Continental army march to the music of a fife and drum.

Meanwhile, about 250 colonists had gathered in Concord, led by Major John Buttrick. They tried not to be afraid of the 700 British soldiers that were headed their way. The colonists marched out of Concord to meet the British, but Major Buttrick soon ordered them to stop. Seeing how outnumbered they were, he told his men to **retreat** to Concord. So both groups of men—the American Patriots and the British troops—marched peacefully into Concord. There was no gunfire or violence, only the music of the Patriots' **fifes** and drums.

For a few hours, the two armies stayed away from each other. The colonists remained on a hill outside town while the British troops entered Concord and began looking for the hidden American supplies. They found little because the colonists had moved most of the weapons to the woods nearby. The British did find some gunpowder, however, and soon they

The British started a fire in Concord using the gunpowder they found there.

used it to start a fire in the town square. The sight of the fire both frightened and angered the American forces. Some of them headed back into town, ready to face the British.

A small group of British soldiers met the Americans at North Bridge. For a moment, there was another stand-off. Then the British began to destroy the bridge to prevent the Americans from crossing it. Suddenly, just as at Lexington, a shot was fired! It was quickly followed by more shots from both sides, and three British soldiers were killed. Several others were wounded, and the British troops soon fled back into Concord.

American Patriots chased British troops across North Bridge.

BACK TO BOSTON

The courage of the Americans surprised Colonel Smith, and he was not sure what to do next. He had been ordered to find the colonists' supplies, but he had not been successful. Should he order his troops to stay in Concord and keep searching? Should he retreat to Boston? For two hours, Smith thought about his decision. Meanwhile, the Patriots gathered more strength. Over the course of the day, news of the battles at Lexington and Concord traveled all over the region, and more Americans left their homes and farms to join the colonial forces. Finally, Smith ordered his men to march back to Boston. What he didn't know was that the Americans were waiting for them.

The British soldiers were well trained, but they had been trained to fight in an orderly way. They were used to facing their enemies across clear battle lines. The American soldiers, however, had learned to fight in a different way.

The British retreating from Concord

When fighting, the Patriots followed the example of Native Americans and surprised their enemies.

Following the example of Native Americans, they learned to surprise their enemies. They hid in the woods and fired when it was least expected.

While retreating through Lexington, the British troops were relieved to see more soldiers arrive under the command of Lord Hugh Percy. He came armed with cannons, and his men fired them to show their strength. One cannonball crashed through the town meetinghouse. Percy ordered his troops to shoot the minutemen and to burn any homes that they used as shelter. To Percy's surprise, however, his men could not find any of the revolutionaries. Every house they entered was empty. This tricky hiding game was successful for the Americans and frustrating for the British.

Lord Hugh Percy and his troops were unable to find the minutemen in Lexington.

As the British continued the march back to Boston, the road was lined on either side with Patriots. They hid behind bushes, trees, hills, and walls. Shots rang out on both sides of the British, and they had nowhere to run. Their bright red coats were perfect targets for the cunning Americans. One by one, the British soldiers began to fall. For almost two hours, the soldiers kept marching, but they lost more and more men as the Patriots kept firing. The British tried to return fire, but the Patriots hid too well. The British felt as though their enemy was invisible— one minute firing, and the next minute disappearing into the woods.

A Patriot fires at British soldiers from a tree where he is hidden from view.

THE REVOLUTION BEGINS

By the time the British reached Boston, it was nearly sunset. They were exhausted and stunned. Never had they dreamed that the Americans would be so strong. In Boston, the British soldiers were safe, armed with warships in Boston Harbor. However, April 19 proved to be a costly day for them. The British had 273 **casualties,** while the Americans only had 95. Today, in the twenty-first century, those numbers may seem low. In 1775, though, they carried huge meaning. The battles at Lexington and Concord had changed the way the British saw the Americans. Those battles had given the Americans courage and determination. No longer did they simply dream of freedom—they were suddenly ready to fight for it.

The following year, as the war with the British continued, the Second Continental Congress took place. At that meeting, a group of men under the leadership of

British warships in Boston Harbor at the beginning of the Revolutionary War

The signing of the Declaration of Independence on July 4, 1776

Thomas Jefferson wrote the Declaration of Independence. That document, signed on July 4, 1776, officially declared American independence from Great Britain. In 1778, France decided to help the American forces and sent soldiers to join in the Revolutionary War. Troops from Poland soon came to America, as well. Several other countries gave the American troops support and encouragement.

The fighting finally ended in 1781, and a peace **treaty** with Britain was signed in 1783. By then, thousands of men on both sides had lost their lives. The British government suffered financial losses. American soldiers, who had spent years away from their farms and businesses, had also lost a great deal. However, what they gained was a dream come true. They gained the freedom to govern themselves. Those first shots fired at Lexington and Concord may have started small battles, but the war that followed changed the world.

A memorial in Lexington is dedicated to the Patriots who lost their lives there at the start of the Revolutionary War.

GLOSSARY

casualties—soldiers killed, wounded, captured or missing in battle

colonies—lands settled by people from another country and ruled by that country

fifes—small musical instruments similar to flutes

massacre—the killing of a large number of helpless people

merchant—a person who buys and sells goods

muskets—guns with long barrels used before rifles were invented

Parliament—the part of the British government that makes laws

Patriots—American colonists who wanted their independence from Britain; patriots are people who love their country

retreat—to move back from a dangerous situation

treaty—an agreement between two governments

DID YOU KNOW?

- When the Revolutionary War began, the population of Great Britain was three times that of the colonies. Great Britain also had the largest navy in the world.

- George Washington served as commander of the Continental army, which was the name of the forces that fought the British. He went on to become the first president of the United States.

- As the first shots were being fired in Lexington and Concord, Benjamin Franklin was sailing home from England. This American statesman and colonial leader had spent ten years there, trying to work out differences between colonial leaders and the British government.

- Paul Revere's actions on the night of April 18, 1775, were the subject of a poem written by Henry Wadsworth Longfellow in 1860. *Paul Revere's Ride* was published the following year in the *Atlantic Monthly* magazine.

43

IMPORTANT DATES

Timeline

1770	The Boston Massacre results in the death of five colonists.
1773	Patriots dump tea into Boston Harbor in what comes to be known as the Boston Tea Party.
1774	The First Continental Congress meets.
1775	On April 18, Paul Revere makes his famous ride to warn people of the British troops' advance; on April 19, the Battles of Lexington and Concord take place.
1776	The Second Continental Congress meets; on July 4, the Declaration of Independence is signed.
1778	French soldiers join the American side in the Revolutionary War.
1781	Fighting ends between British troops and the colonists.
1783	Great Britain and the United States sign the Treaty of Paris.

IMPORTANT PEOPLE

SAMUEL ADAMS

(1722–1803), *Patriot who led opposition to British rule of the colonies*

JOHN BUTTRICK

(1715–1791), *major who led the colonists at Concord*

THOMAS GAGE

(1721–1787), *British general who was ordered to find and destroy American supplies in Concord*

JOHN HANCOCK

(1737–1793), *leader of the Patriot cause*

LORD HUGH PERCY

(1742–1817), *British soldier who led troops at Lexington*

JOHN PARKER

(1758–1844), *captain who led the Patriots at Lexington*

JOHN PITCAIRN

(1740?–1775), *British major who led troops at Lexington*

PAUL REVERE

(1734–1818), *Patriot messenger whose famous ride warned colonists of the British troops' advance*

WANT TO KNOW MORE?

At the Library

Grote, Joann A. *Paul Revere: American Patriot.* Broomall, Pa.: Chelsea
House, 1999.

Kallen, Stuart A. *Samuel Adams.* Edina, Minn.: Abdo & Daughters, 2002.

Kent, Deborah. *Lexington and Concord.* Danbury, Conn.: Children's
Press, 1998.

Peacock, Judith. *The Battles of Lexington and Concord.* Mankato, Minn.:
Bridgestone Books, 2002.

On the Web

For more information on this topic, use FactHound.

1. Go to *www.facthound.com*

2. Type in this book ID: 0756504902

3. Click on the *Fetch It* button.

FactHound will find the best Web sites for you.

Through the Mail

Concord Museum

200 Lexington Road

Concord, MA 01742

978/369-9763

To receive information about the Revolutionary War and to see one of the lanterns used in the signal Paul Revere arranged

On the Road

Minute Man National Historical Park

174 Liberty Street

Concord, MA 01742

978/369-6993

To see where the Battle of Concord took place

The Paul Revere House

19 North Square

Boston, MA 02113

617/523-2338

To visit Paul Revere's historic home

INDEX

About the Author

Lucia Raatma received her bachelor's degree in English literature from the University of South Carolina and her master's degree in cinema studies from New York University. She has written a wide range of books for young people. When she is not researching or writing, she enjoys going to movies, playing tennis, practicing yoga, and spending time with her husband, daughter, and golden retriever. She lives in New York.